Bearwood

on old pic

Andre..

GREETINGS FROM BEARWOOD

Warley Woods, Golf Links, Smethwick.

Windsor Theatre, Bearwood Road, Smethwick.

The Hall and New Pool, Lightwoods Park, Smethwick.

Smethwick Baths.

1. "Greetings from Bearwood" on a multi-view postcard published about 1930 by Elsie Phelps, Stationer & Post Office of Upper St. Mary's Road, Bearwood. The 'Windsor Theatre' became an ice rink and is now a snooker centre.

£3.50

INTRODUCTION

Both the popular residential areas of Warley and Bearwood are now under Sandwell Borough Council in the West Midlands. Before this, Warley was in Worcestershire and Bearwood in Staffordshire (though on the Warwickshire border).

Warley, as part of the Southern area of Oldbury, remained very rural until as recently as the 1920's. However in 1928, a large area (including the landscaped Warley Woods Park) was transferred from Oldbury to Smethwick County Borough for housing development. By World War Two, the area was almost entirely residential. Fortunately, Warley Woods has survived, and with the help of National Lottery money, looks set to prosper.

Bearwood also was a rural area until the 1880's, with small settlements around the 'Bear Inn' (known to exist by 1718) and the 'Old King's Head' (now Quantum). It developed rapidly as a residential area in the late 1800's and early 1900's, and an important shopping centre grew up along the southern part of Bearwood Road.

Regrettably, in 1997 the Royal Mail advised Warley and Bearwood residents that their address was now to be just Smethwick, despite the fact that Bearwood and Warley are distinctive areas in their own right. Smethwick itself has been well documented in other similar publications; this book is not intended to be a complete history of the two areas, but more a nostalgic look at some of the buildings, streets, pubs, parks and shops. Also featured is a series of views taking us down Bearwood Road from the 'Bear Inn' to the 'King's Head' on Hagley Road.

The first picture postcard in Britain was published in 1894, but it was not until a decade later that they began to take off, when in 1902 the Post Office allowed a message to be written on the address side. This meant that the whole of one side was available for the picture, and this obviously gave more scope to the publishers. Photographic viewcards became very popular, and a national craze by 1905 saw the postcard become the most important way of communicating news or messages, in much the same way as the telephone is used today. The years up to 1914 were the "Golden Age" of picture postcards, when countless millions of imaginative designs, covering every subject under the sun, were published by a host of national and local firms. There's hardly a village or hamlet that wasn't documented at that time by a postcard publisher. Postcard collecting declined after World War I, but is once again a growing hobby, with increasing numbers of people taking up this absorbing interest.

Fortunately for us today, Warley and Bearwood were well covered by postcard publishers (especially Warley Woods and Lightwoods Park). There were a number of excellent local photographers whose work allows us a fascinating insight into life in Warley and Bearwood nearly a century ago. They include Howard Cooper of 19 Bearwood Road; Henry John Carless of 5 Wigorn Road; Frank Nightingale, 30 Durban Road, later of 370 Bearwood Road; and William Hutt of 374 Dudley Road. Birmingham photographers Adams & Co ("ADCO"), George Lewis and A.T. Ryberg also operated in the area. National publishers included Lilywhite and Doncaster Rotophoto (both from Yorkshire) and Valentine & Son of Dundee.

I hope you will enjoy this selection of postcards as much as I have enjoyed assembling them for this book.

My thanks go to Smethwick Library and their excellent local history section; Birmingham Library Services (no. 52 reproduced by kind permission); Yvonne Edkins, and David Yates, whose wealth of knowledge has been invaluable.

Andrew Maxam
March 2000

Dedication:
For Estelle, Rachel and Rosemary.

2. Warley and Lightwoods Park Smethwick on a multi-view postcard published in Hallam's series, and sent to Co. Donegal in March 1935.

Designed and published by
Reflections of a Bygone Age,
Keyworth, Nottingham 2000

Printed by Adlard Print
& Reprographics Ltd

Front cover: Bearwood Road just before the First World War, showing 'The Bear' pub and Bearwood School Tower on the left, and George Moss's ironmonger's shop on the right. No publisher is named on this postcard, posted to Glasgow in June 1914. *"They are a very good class of shop,"* wrote the sender.

3. The Warley Bowl on a card published by W.G.Alford of Quinton c.1967.

4. Wolverhampton Road, Warley, on a postcard published by Richards of York, postally used in 1939. Harold Goodwin's motor showroom, on the right, is now long gone and McDonalds now occupies the site. The centre row of shops now house Jonathan's restaurant, and the low, triangular roofed building is now Lightwoods Post Office.

5. Wolverhampton Road, Warley, on a card used in 1966. The water tower near Warley Woods can be seen (far left), as can the junction with Castle Road East (centre).

6. Beech Lanes Baptist Chapel on a postcard published by Howard Cooper c.1905, showing a Temperance Society parade. The Chapel was built in 1824 and, after use as an auction room, is now demolished.

7. Another view of the parade, with the banners proclaiming *"Temperance Little Darlings"* and *"Strong Drink Weaves the Net of Poverty"*. Note the 'Cock and Magpies' pub in the background (right). A new chapel was opened in Castle Road East in 1935.

8. The 'George Hotel' in Warley on a postcard published by Scott Russell & Co. of Birmingham, posted in 1913 to Ipswich. Then Albert Edwards was the licensee at this now rebuilt pub in George Road.

9. The 'Pheasant Inn,' Warley, showing the old building in Abbey Road, before it was replaced by the current larger premises in 1938. Some of the old wall (right) still remains today.

10. Harborne Road, Warley Woods c.1960. Grove Road leads off to the right.

Water Tower & Golf Course, Warley.

11. Water Tower & Golf Course, Warley c.1960. This photograph was taken from the golf course looking towards Harborne Road. The Water Tower was built in 1939.

THE LODGE LIGHTWOODS HILL ENTRANCE TO WARLEY PARK - N°8

12. The Lodge, Lightwoods Hill, showing the entrance to Warley Park, on a card published locally by Henry Carless c.1908. A plaque on the now-demolished lodge reads *"County Police Station"*.

13. Warley Golf Links, Warley Woods, on a 1935 postcard by unidentified publisher. The card shows golf professional A.J. Padgham in action on the course.

14. Boy Scouts Rally, Warley Woods Park, 17th July 1909. General Baden-Powell was present in the motor car (centre right), watching the sports.

WARLEY WOODS OPENING DAY

15. Warley Woods Opening Day on another postcard by Carless. The park was officially

pened to the public on 9th June 1906.

16. Warley Abbey on a postcard published by H.J. Carless of Bearwood and postally used in 1911. Landowner Samuel Galton's son, Hubert, built the Abbey in 1819, and the estate passed to Birmingham Corporation in 1906. The Abbey was demolished in 1957.

"NEW PART" WARLEY WOODS PARK

17. New Part, Warley Woods Park, on a card dating from 1913, and posted to Jersey in August of that year. The golf course now occupies this part of the park, and it seems incredible that sheep used to graze here!

18. Barclay Road, Warley, on a card published by George Lewis, used in 1917, showing Abbey Road Junior School (right).

19. Barclay Road School, Warley Woods, in1905 on a card by Carless, showing the Junior School. The photo was taken from where Maurice Road is now.

TELFORD CLOSE WARLEY. BIRD'S SERIES

20. Telford Close, Warley, on a card published by George Bird at the sub-post office at 162 Abbey Road. The card was used in 1945.

Oldbury Urban District Council Election

WARLEY—South Ward.

Polling Day—MONDAY, APRIL 7th, 1913.

Mr. Arthur F. Shaw

requests the favour of your

Vote and Interest.

The Candidate with over 15 years' experience in the carrying out of Public Work.

Printed by James Baldwin & Sons, Ltd., Morville St., Birmingham.

21. Arthur F. Shaw election postcard of 1913. He stood in the Council Election for the Warley South Ward, an election that he went on to win.

SMETHWICK NEW BATHS, BEARWOOD. "Express Series" No. A 66

22. Smethwick New Baths, Bearwood, on a card published in the "Express Series," postally used in 1937. The swimming baths at Thimblemill Road were opened in 1933.

23. An interior view of Smethwick Baths, Thimblemill Road. This was an advertising card used by a building firm to show an example of their work.

24. The 'Thimblemill' public house, Thimblemill Road, about 1930. It is still the same today.

25. Katherine Road, Bearwood, was developed by William Henry Jones, who occupied Slatch House Farm, and named the road after his wife. Other roads in the area were named after his family members.

26. Abbey Road, Bearwood, on a postcard published by Thornely Brothers, newsagents, at 21 Abbey Road, in 1913. This fine card shows Alfred Street's confectioner's shop at no. 28 (far left); David Jones, baker & confectioner's cart (centre - based at no. 37) and F. Day, greengrocer's cart of no. 33 Abbey Road.

27. St. Hilda's Church, Rathbone Road, on a card also published by Thornely Brothers, and sent in 1938. This view looks to the junction with Abbey Road and Galton Road. The Church has now been demolished.

ABBEY RD. BEARWOOD.

28. Abbey Road, Bearwood, on a card by Birmingham publisher Adams & Co. Katherin

ad can be seen on the left.

29. Park Road, Bearwood, looking towards Lightwoods Park, on a card sent to Small Heath in 1914.

30. Wigorn Road, Bearwood, on a card published as part of the *"Rambles in Bearwood"* series, 1915. This view is looking towards the Lightwoods Hill/ Adkins Lane island. Local photographer Henry Carless lived at no. 5 (left).

31. Milcote Road, Bearwood, taken from the Adkins Lane end. Not a car in sight on this postcard, sent to Glasgow in 1914. *"I have marked in ink the house I am staying in,"* wrote the sender.

32. Upper St. Mary's Road, Bearwood, on a card published by Frank Nightingale of Smethwick, used in 1912. Katherine Lewis, beer retailer, is on the corner of Park Road (left), where an off-licence still remains.

ST MARY'S RD. BEARWOOD.

33. Upper St. Mary's Road, Bearwood, at the junction with Galton Road (centre), looking down from Barclay Road.

COPYRIGHT BHM/SK6.

BEARWOOD ROAD, FROM THREE SHIRES OAK ROAD,
LOOKING SOUTH, SMETHWICK.

LILYWHITE LTD.,
THE PHOTO PRINTERS.

34. Bearwood Road from Three Shires Oak Road, looking south, on a card by national publisher Lilywhite Ltd. This card shows the 'Bear Inn' (right) c1920.

35. 'The Bear Inn,' Bearwood, on a postcard sent to Leamington Spa in 1904. This card shows 'The Bear' before it was rebuilt in 1906. Note the tower in the distance, which formed part of Bearwood Road school before being bombed in World War Two.

36. Bearwood Road on a card used in 1927, showing the London Joint City & Midland Bank (now HSBC).

37. Bearwood Road on a card used in 1905 and published locally by Howard Cooper. The bank. *"My dear Maud,"* wrote Frank, *"you will see on the photo that our shop is on th*

utcher's shop at the corner of Rutland Road (right) has now been rebuilt and is Lloyds TSB
ft side of the street."

38. Bearwood Road, Smethwick, published in the "Challenge Series," posted to Portsmouth in June 1910. Note the United Counties Bank (now Barclays) at the corner of Rutland Road.

39. Bearwood Road, Bearwood, on a postcard by national publisher Doncaster Rotophoto Co. Ltd, used in 1934. Looking at the junction with Sherwood Road (left), the triangular roof of St. Mary's Church can be seen (centre left). Also note the Midland Red bus depot & head office (right), since 1979 the site of Safeway supermarket.

40. Bearwood Road at the junction with Anderson Road (right), still known as Warley Road at this time. Card published by A.T. Ryberg of Birmingham and used in 1913.

41. Bearwood Road, Smethwick, on a postcard published by Valentine & Sons Ltd of Dundee c.1960. 40 years later, just Woolworths (centre left) and Bradbury's shops remain from this viewpoint. Note the "Midland" sign on the old bus depot.

BEARWOOD AD. SMETHWICK

42. Bearwood Road, Smethwick, on a superb card by William Hutt in 1908, showing som
sold Cheshire Ales, brewed in Smethwick.

ouses now converted to shops. The off-licence (right), at the junction with Poplar Road,

Smethwick Telephone Series.   BEARWOOD (SMETHWICK.)   H. Cooper, Photo.

43. Bearwood (Smethwick) on a card published by the local newspaper, the *Smethwick Telephone*, in 1905. This photo by Howard Cooper was taken from the Hagley Road end, showing the houses (left) before they were converted into shops. The card was posted locally in March 1905.

44. Birmingham Corporation Tramway's no. 179 at the Bearwood Road 29 route terminus near Adkins Lane c.1915. Trams ran down Bearwood Road to Birmingham city centre via Cape Hill until the line was abandoned in 1939. Note George Mason's provision merchant's shop at no. 624, and the British & Argentine Meat Co., butcher's, at 622 Bearwood Road.

45. The Tram Terminus, Bearwood, on a card published by Doncaster Rotophoto in the early 1920's. The Hagley Road route no. 34 terminated here outside the 'King's Head' public house, until abandoned in 1930.

46. Beech Lanes. An early postcard published by Howard Cooper showing the old 'Kings Head' (left), demolished in 1903 and replaced by the current building, at the Lordswood Road/ Bearwood Road crossroads with Hagley Road West (then called Beech Lanes). This quiet scene is now an extremely busy junction, and only the row of shops (far right) remains today.

47. Hagley Road West, after the trams had finished and a traffic island had been installed c.1932.

743   BIRMINGHAM CITY POLICE BAND   THE HUDSON STUDIOS LTD. B'HAM

48. Birmingham City Police Band, published by Hudson of Birmingham, outside Lightwoods Hall, Lightwoods Park c.1920.

49. Continental Tea Gardens, Lightwoods Park, c.1908. A rare view inside Lightwoods Hall. Note the prominent Cadburys Cocoa posters

50. Lightwoods Park pool c.1908 on a card by William Hutt. A rural view of the park, complete with wooden rustic bridge (centre). It is now occupied by the children's playground.

51. Beech Lanes, near The 'King's Head', on a card used in 1923. Now this is the busy, widened Hagley Road West. On the left is Lightwoods Park.

52. Hagley Road West looking out of town, with the 'New Talbot' public house (right) at the junction with Anderson Road c.1930.

53. Poplar Road, Bearwood, on a card published by Frank Nightingale of Birmingham in 1912. Drayton Road can be seen off to the right.

54. Hagley Road, at the junction with Barnsley Road, on a card sent to France in 1917. The horse is pulling a cart owned by Goodyears Machine Bakery of Bearwood Road.

55. Sandon Road, Edgbaston, about 1917, showing the row of houses from the junction with City Road, just outside Bearwood's boundary with Edgbaston.

56. Sandon Road, Bearwood, showing the Wesleyan Chapel, now Sandon Road Family Church. The card was posted to a patient in Birmingham General Hospital in January 1911.

57. In Lightwoods Park on a card used in 1912, showing Lightwoods Hall.